GARY SOTO

A FIRE IN MY HANDS

A BOOK OF POEMS

SCHOLASTIC HARDCOVER

Scholastic Inc.
New York

Cover painting and illustrations by James M. Cardillo

ACKNOWLEDGMENTS

Grateful acknowledgment is made to the following publishers and author for permission to reprint copyrighted material.

Chronicle Books for "That Girl" and "Evening Walk" from WHO WILL KNOW US? Copyright © 1990 by Gary Soto. Reprinted by permission of the publisher.

The Modern Poetry Association for "Hitchhiking With a Friend and a Book That Explains the Pacific Ocean" by Gary Soto. From WHERE SPARROWS WORK HARD by Gary Soto. First appeared in POETRY © 1981 by The Modern Poetry Association. Reprinted by permission of the Editor of POETRY and Gary Soto.

Gary Soto for "Where We Could Go" from BLACK HAIR © 1985 by Gary Soto. Reprinted by permission of the author.

University of Pittsburgh Press for "October." Reprinted from THE ELEMENTS OF SAN JOAQUIN, by Gary Soto, by permission of the University of Pittsburgh Press. © 1977 by Gary Soto. For "In August," "Autumn With a Daughter Who's Just Catching On," "Black Hair," "Oranges," "Brown Girl, Blonde Okie," "Learning to Bargain," "Heaven," "How to Sell Things," "Kearney Park," "Morning on This Street," "Envying the Children of San Francisco," "Failing in the Presence of Ants," "Pepper Tree," "Eating Bread," "Finding a Lucky Number," "Teaching Numbers," "How Things Work" and "Looking Around, Believing." Reprinted from BLACK HAIR, by Gary Soto, by permission of the University of Pittsburgh Press. © 1985 by Gary Soto.

Library of Congress Cataloging-in-Publication Data

Soto, Gary.
A fire in my hands : a book of poems / Gary Soto.
p.   cm.

ISBN 0-590-45021-2

I. Title.

PS3569.072F5 1991
811'.54 — dc20

91-11669
CIP

12 11 10 9 8 7 6 5 4 3 2 1   11   1 2 3 4 5 6/9
Printed in the U.S.A.   37

CONTENTS

To my teacher, Philip Levine

FOREWORD

I began writing poems fifteen years ago while I was in college. One day I was in the library, working on a term paper, when by chance I came across an anthology of contemporary poetry. I don't remember the title of the book or any of the titles of the poems except one: "Frankenstein's Daughter." The poem was wild, almost rude, and nothing like the rhyme-and-meter poetry I had read in high school. I had always thought that poetry was flowery writing about sunsets and walks on the beach, but that library book contained a direct and sometimes shocking poetry about dogs, junked cars, rundown houses, and TVs. I checked the book out, curious to read more.

Soon afterward, I started filling a notebook with my own poems. At first I was scared, partly because my poetry teacher, to whom this book is dedicated, was a stern man who could see the errors in my poems. Also, I realized the seriousness of my dedication. I gave up geography to study poetry, which a good many friends said offered no future. I ignored them because I liked working with words, using them to reconstruct the past, which has always been a source of poetry for me.

When I first studied poetry, I was single-minded. I woke to poetry and went to bed with poetry. I memorized poems, read English poets because I was told they would help shape my poems, and read classical Chinese poetry because I was told that it would add clarity to my work. But I was most taken by Spanish and Latin American poets, particularly Pablo Neruda. My favorites of his were the odes — long,

short-lined poems celebrating common things like toma-
toes, socks, scissors, and artichokes. I felt joyful when I read
these odes; and when I began to write my own poems, I tried
to remain faithful to the common things of my
childhood — dogs, alleys, my baseball mitt, curbs, and the
fruit of the valley, especially the orange. I wanted to give
these things life, to write so well that my poems would
express their simple beauty.

I also admired our own country's poetry. I saw that our
poets often wrote about places where they grew up or places
that impressed them deeply. James Wright wrote about
Ohio and West Virginia, Philip Levine about Detroit, Gary
Snyder about the Sierra Nevadas and about Japan, where for
years he studied Zen Buddhism. I decided to write about the
San Joaquin Valley, where my hometown, Fresno, is located.
Some of my poems are stark observations of human
violence — burglaries, muggings, fistfights — while
others are spare images of nature — the orange groves and
vineyards, the Kings River, the bogs, the Sequoias. I fell in
love with the valley, both its ugliness and its beauty, and
quietly wrote poems about it to share with others.

I like to think of my poems as a "working life," by which I
mean that my poems are about commonplace, everyday
things — baseball, an evening walk, a boyhood friendship,
first love, fatherhood, a tree, rock 'n' roll, the homeless,
dancing. The poems keep alive the small moments which
add up to a large moment: life itself.

Fifteen years. I had no idea that I would write so much or
that more than a few friends would read what I wrote. Some
of you will read these poems and will want to write your
own. Good. Poems should feed into other poems — a nee-

dle passing a stitch through cloth. My advice to young poets is "Look to your own lives." What are your life stories? Can you remember incidents from your childhood? Some of you will say that your lives are boring, that nothing has happened, that everything interesting happens far away. Not so. Your lives are at work, too.

Each of the twenty-three poems in this collection is preceded by an anecdote. In the back of the book, I answer questions about poetry. Your answers one day may differ from mine. Each poet works differently. But the task is always the same — to get the language right so that the subject of the poem will live.

Gary Soto
August 1989

As a kid, I was no good at baseball. Many of my summers were spent watching games from the bleachers and rooting for a player who was Mexican, like me.

BLACK HAIR

At eight I was brilliant with my body.
In July, that ring of heat
We all jumped through, I sat in the bleachers
Of Romain Playground, in the lengthening
Shade that rose from our dirty feet.
The game before us was more than baseball.
It was a figure — Hector Moreno
Quick and hard with turned muscles,
His crouch the one I assumed before an altar
Of worn baseball cards, in my room.

I came here because I was Mexican, a stick
Of brown light in love with those
Who could do it — the triple and hard slide,
The gloves eating balls into double plays.
What could I do with 50 pounds, my shyness,
My black torch of hair, about to go out?
Father was dead, his face no longer
Hanging over the table or our sleep,
And mother was the terror of mouths
Twisting hurt by butter knives.

In the bleachers I was brilliant with my body,
Waving players in and stomping my feet,

Growing sweaty in the presence of white shirts.
I chewed sunflower seeds. I drank water
And bit my arm through the late innings.
When Hector lined balls into deep
Center, in my mind I rounded the bases
With him, my face flared, my hair lifting
Beautifully, because we were coming home
To the arms of brown people.

Once, when I caught a friend hurting a cat, I threatened to tell his mom if he didn't stop. He stopped because he knew that his mother would scold him, or worse. This poem grew out of that experience.

LEARNING TO BARGAIN

Summer. Flies knitting
Filth on the window,
A mother calling a son home . . .
I'm at that window, looking
Onto the street: dusk,
A neighbor kid sharpening
A stick at the curb.
I go outside and sit
Next to him without saying
A word. When he looks
Up, his eyes dark as flies . . .
I ask about the cat, the one dead
Among the weeds in the alley.
"Yeah, I did it," he admits,
And stares down at his feet,
Then my feet. "What do you want?"
"A dime," I say. Without
Looking at me, he gets
Up, goes behind his house,
And returns with two Coke bottles.
"These make a dime." He sits
At the curb, his shoulders
So bony they could be wings
To lift him so far. "Don't tell."
He snaps a candy into halves
And we eat in silence.

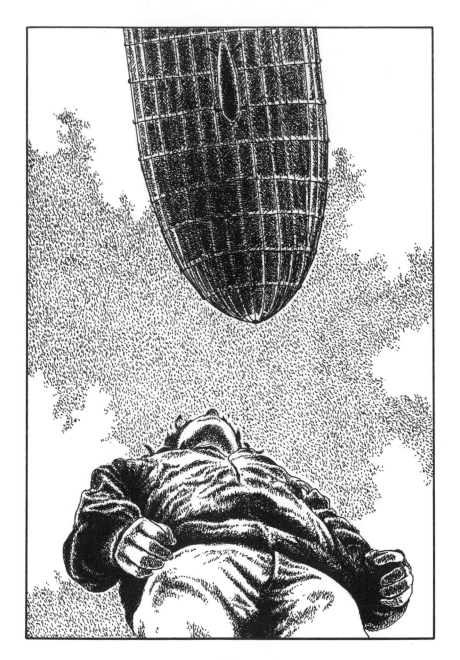

One summer day I looked up and saw a blimp hovering above me at the pickle factory near our home. My friends and I were not allowed there, but because it was a Saturday, we thought we had the run of the yard.

IN AUGUST

A blimp was above me
And then gone,
Like all I would ever know.
Like father with hands in my hair.
Like uncle on the porch with his arms
And little else. I walked
In the alley looking up
Until it wasn't the sky before
Me, but a plum tree,
Its dark fruit, notched and open
Where birds ate. I climbed
Into it, searched, dropped
With two in each hand.
I walked from the alley
To Coleman Pickle
Where brother, friends, tiny sister
Were standing in barrels,
Pickles in their hands
And saying, they're good,
Better than plums. I climbed

Into a barrel and fished for one
— came up to see the blimp
Pass quietly as a cloud,
Its shadow dark enough to sleep
Or dream in. We watched
It, with food in our mouths,
All wondering, until it was above us
And then gone,
Like all we would ever know.

When I first started liking girls, about the time I was thirteen and in seventh grade, I often couldn't concentrate on my homework, which I did at the public library. I would look up, and there would be a girl I could like.

THAT GIRL

The public library was saying things
In so many books,
And I, Catholic boy
In a green sweater,
Was reading the same page
A hundred times.
A girl was in my way,
Protestant or Jew.
And she was at the other end
Of the oak table,
Her hands like doves
On the encyclopedia, E–G.
England, I thought,
Germany before the war?
She'll copy from that book,
Cursive like waves
Riding to the shore,
And tomorrow walk across lawns
In a public school dress
With no guilt pulling at an ear.
And me? I'll kick
My Catholic shoes through
Leaves, stand in the

Cloakroom and eat
A friend's lunch. My work
Was never finished.
My maps were half-colored,
History a stab in the dark,
And fractions the inside
Of a pocket watch
Spilled on my desk.
I was no good. And who do I
Blame? That girl.
When she scribbled a pink
Eraser and her pony
Tails bounced like skirts,
I looked up, gazed for what
My mother and sister could not
Offer, then returned to
The same sentence: *The Nile*
Is the longest river in the world.
A pencil rolled from the
Table when she clicked open
Her binder. I looked up,
Gazed, looked back down:
The Nile is the longest river . . .

Occasionally our family had picnics at a riverbend called Piedra. The water was swift and the mountains cold with shadows, especially at the beginning of winter.

OCTOBER

A cold day, though only October,
And the grass has grayed
Like the frost that hardened it
This morning.

        And this morning
After the wind left
With its pile of clouds
The broken fence steamed, sunlight spread
Like seed from one field
To another, out of a bare sycamore
Sparrows lifted above the ridge.

In the ditch an owl shuffled into a nest
Of old leaves and cotton,
A black tassel of lizard flapping
From its beak. Mice
And ants gathered under the flat ground
And slipped downward like water,
A coyote squatted behind granite,
His ears tilting
Toward a rustle, eyes dark
With winter to come.

I never received an allowance. If I wanted money for a movie or a popsicle, I had to earn it. Often I went from door to door selling oranges.

HOW TO SELL THINGS

First, you need a dog
Chased hungry by a cloud
All night, fur over
His eyes, breath white
In the early morning
That has sent you door
To door with a sack
Of oranges. Two for
A nickel, you might say,
Two for a dime if it's
A grandma who's known
Steak and roses in her time.
Play it up. Backhand
Your nose, shiver like a leaf,
And look down at shoes
That were once cows at
The turn of the century.
A hard grandma? Then
Call the dog to roll over,
Whine, and raise a paw.
If the grandma is still
With hands on hips
And shaking her head,

Then call on the dog
To speak a few words
On his back — tiny feet
Prancing in the air.
Make sure it's Sunday
When God is looking around
For something to do.

I don't know if you can call it a "date" or not, but the first girl who allowed me to walk with her was named Margie. I couldn't think of anything to do but walk around the block three or four times.

ORANGES

The first time I walked
With a girl, I was twelve,
Cold, and weighted down
With two oranges in my jacket.
December. Frost cracking
Beneath my steps, my breath
Before me, then gone,
As I walked toward
Her house, the one whose
Porch light burned yellow
Night and day, in any weather.
A dog barked at me, until
She came out pulling
At her gloves, face bright
With rouge. I smiled,
Touched her shoulder, and led
Her down the street, across
A used car lot and a line
Of newly planted trees,
Until we were breathing
Before a drugstore. We
Entered, the tiny bell
Bringing a saleslady
Down a narrow aisle of goods.
I turned to the candies
Tiered like bleachers,
And asked what she wanted —

Light in her eyes, a smile
Starting at the corners
Of her mouth. I fingered
A nickel in my pocket,
And when she lifted a chocolate
That cost a dime,
I didn't say anything.
I took the nickel from
My pocket, then an orange,
And set them quietly on
The counter. When I looked up,
The lady's eyes met mine,
And held them, knowing
Very well what it was all
About.

          Outside,
A few cars hissing past,
Fog hanging like old
Coats between the trees.
I took my girl's hand
In mine for two blocks,
Then released it to let
Her unwrap the chocolate.
I peeled my orange
That was so bright against
The gray of December
That, from some distance,
Someone might have thought
I was making a fire in my hands.

Jackie was a childhood friend. One summer evening we sat on the grass talking about who we were going to end up marrying. Each of us had a clear notion of what made a girl beautiful, and each of us thought the other wrong.

BROWN GIRL, BLONDE OKIE

Jackie and I cross-legged
In the yard, plucking at
Grass, cupping flies
And shattering them against
Each other's faces —
Smiling that it's summer,
No school, and we can
Sleep out under stars
And the blink of jets
Crossing up our lives.
The flies leave, or die,
And we are in the dark,
Still cross-legged,
Talking not dogs or baseball,
But whom will we love,
What brown girl or blonde
Okie to open up to
And say we are sorry
For our faces, the filth
We shake from our hair,
The teeth without direction.
"We're ugly," says Jackie
On one elbow, and stares

Lost between jets
At what this might mean.
In the dark I touch my
Nose, trace my lips, and pinch
My mouth into a dull flower.
Oh God, we're in trouble.

In late 1964, the British invasion took place. I'm not speaking about a military invasion, but the landing of The Beatles and The Rolling Stones. They were unbelievable. They made us so happy that we nearly ruined our beds from jumping up and down on them.

HEAVEN

Scott and I bent
To the radio, legs
Twitching to The Stones,
Faces wet, arms rising
And falling as if
Trying to get out or
Crawl the air — the
Air thick with our
Toweled smells.

It's
'64, and our room
And its shaft of dust,
Turning, is all
There is — though Mamma
Says there's the car
To wash, the weeds,
The grass and garbage
Tilting on the back steps.
"Yeh, yeh," we scream
Behind the closed door,
And boost the radio
To "10" and begin

Bouncing on the bed,
Singing, making up
Words about this girl,
That car, tears,
Lipstick, handjives
In alleys — bouncing
Hard, legs split, arms
Open for the Lord,
Until Scott can't stand it
And crashes through
The screened window
And tumbles into a bush,
His shoulders locked
Between branches,
His forehead scratched,
But still singing,
"Baby, baby, o baby."

I happened to grow up in a flat house in a very flat town. After watching a 1940's movie about a genteel family living in a tall apartment building in a large, hill-rolling city, I yearned to live in a tall apartment building in a hill-rolling city, too. While we had three front steps that carried us to noisy television, they had an elevator that carried them to the twelfth floor and a good view of the world.

ENVYING THE CHILDREN OF SAN FRANCISCO

At a city square
Children laugh in the red
Sweaters of Catholics,
As they walk home between trucks
And sunlight angled off buildings that end in points.
I'm holding an apple, among shoppers
Clutching bags big enough to sleep in,
And the air is warm for October —
Torn pieces of paper
Scuttling like roaches, a burst at a time.

The children are blond,
Shiny, and careful at the lights —
The sister with her brother's hand.
They cross looking
At their watches, and I cross too.
I want to know where
They're going, what door they'll push
Open and call home —
The TV coming on,
Milk, a cookie for each hand.

As a kid I wanted to live
In the city, in a building that rose above it all,
The gray streets burst open, a rattle
Of jackhammers. I wanted to
Stare down from the eighteenth floor, and let things go —
My homework for one, a paper plane
With a half-drawn heart and a girl's name.
I wanted to say that I ate
And slept, ate and slept in a building
That faced other buildings, a sliver of sea
Blue in the distance.

I wanted to hear voices
Behind walls, the *click-click* of a poodle
Strolling to his bowl — a violin like fingers
Running down a blackboard.
I wanted to warm my hands at a teakettle
And comb my hair in an elevator, my mouth
Still rolling with cereal, as I started off
For school, a row of pens in my shirt pocket.
Back home at the window
I wanted it to be December —
Flags and honking cars,
A Santa Claus with his pot, a single red
Balloon let go and racing skyward,
And the tiny mothers who would come around
Buildings, disappear, and come around again,
Hugging bags for all they were worth to children.

One Sunday my girlfriend and I came across dancers while we were walking through a park. We joined them, shyly at first, because we didn't know how to dance very well. But in no time we were kicking up our heels to the music.

KEARNEY PARK

True Mexicans or not, let's open our shirts
And dance, a spark of heels
Chipping at the dusty cement. The people
Are shiny like the sea, turning
To the clockwork of rancheras,
The accordion wheezing, the drum-tap
Of work rising and falling.
Let's dance with our hats in hand.
The sun is behind the trees,
Behind my stutter of awkward steps
With a woman who is a brilliant arc of smiles,
An armful of falling water. Her skirt
Opens and closes. My arms
Know no better but to flop
On their own, and we spin, dip
And laugh into each other's faces —
Faces that could be famous
On the coffee table of my abuelita.
But grandma is here, at the park, with a beer
At her feet, clapping
And shouting, "Dance, hijo, dance!"
Laughing, I bend, slide, and throw up
A great cloud of dust,
Until the girl and I are no more.

One day a friend and I decided to hitchhike to the ocean. We were young men in need of adventure. When we were left off on the side of a road, the wind-swept field seemed strangely familiar, yet new, and the gray sky, haunting. We walked over the crunch of gravel, feeling utterly free at being far from home.

HITCHHIKING WITH A FRIEND AND A BOOK THAT EXPLAINS THE PACIFIC OCEAN

On 41, outside Straford,
The sky lengthens magically
When you're 19, the first time
On the road — and if you're
With a friend, the birds lift
And never come down in the same place.
I found myself out there, with Samuel,
Hungry as a fire, kicking rocks,
Under clouds giving up
Just as we came to believe in beauty.
It was that word, and others,
That had us pointing
To windmills and sullen cows,
The trees irresponsible with their shadows.
And it was the eagerness of grass
Under wind, a tumbleweed
Moving, a paper bag moving,
And our minds clear as water
Pooled on roadsides. We went
On for hours. The gravel

Turned under our march,
Until the landscape meant less,
And we grew tired. A banged
Truck stopped for us
And the driver's giddy dog licked
And nuzzled our necks
All through the foothills, toward Pismo Beach.
Two hours, two beers, and the sky
Hazed with mist. When we saw
A rough cut of sea through trees,
We tilted our heads, nudged each
Other's ribs, at the blue
Of waves that would end at our feet.

Where we lived, there were few homeless people. I do remember, however, a man in overalls who used to pull his wife on a cart. She sat hunched under a makeshift canopy. All the kids stopped playing when they passed.

MORNING ON THIS STREET

It's Saturday with the gray
Noise of rain at the window,
Its fingers weeping to get in.
We're in bunk beds, one brother
Talking football, another
Turning to the dreamed girl
He'd jump from a tree to die for.
Later, in the kitchen,
He tells me, Love is like snow
Or something. I listen
With a bowl at the stove, dress,
And go outside to trees dripping
Rain, a pickup idling
With its headlights on.
I look for something to do
Slowly with a stick
In the absence of love,
That Catholic skirt in a pew.
I walk banging fences
Until Earl the Cartman rattles
Onto our block — a rope over
His shoulder. He pulls hard

Because his wife, centered
On that cart, is cold
Under the rough temple
Of cardboard he's cut for her.
Her legs are bundled in strips
Of white cloth, half there
With the dead, half with us
Who have oranges to give,
As he steps heavily toward
The trees they'll call
Home — a small fire and the black
Haunt of smoke. It's for his wife
That he lives and pulls a rope
To its frayed end. The sky
Is nothing and these neighbors
Wincing behind windows
Are even less. This is marriage,
A man and a woman, in one kind of weather.

The first word our daughter spoke was flower. *She pointed to a tree, and although a tree is no flower, I knew that it was only a matter of time before she would learn the names of things . . . and more than that.*

AUTUMN WITH A DAUGHTER WHO'S JUST CATCHING ON

You were going to wear red,
Me blue-green, instead we went
To the park in browns. It's easy
To fool the sparrows in such
Colors, if there's bread to
Saucer under gaunt trees.
And that's what we did. The birds
Dropped hints at our feet
And stared at our hands.
They had no idea we were the ones
Who had cut through mountains
And done in the sea,
That we had roughed up rocks
And bruised the sky with smoke.
They hopped in grass; they poked
At leaves and beat their wings
In the dust. Not knowing us,
They made noises so we might love
Them, and toss more than bread.

As a young father, I was always in search of things to do with our daughter. I would take her to a zoo, a playground, a story hour at the library. For the first four years of her life, I was busy taking her places.

WHERE WE COULD GO

Happy that this is another
Country, we're going to
Sit before coffees and croissants
On Rue Lucerne
And watch the working fathers
Labor up the street,
A stiff loaf of bread
In each roughed-up hand.
Some nod to us;
Others pass with the moist eyes
Of a strict wind.
This is France, daughter.
This is the autumn of calendars.
The sparrows are like
Those back home fighting
With the lawn,
Squealing and transparent
As their hunger.
They play at our feet,
Then climb to our knees
To hop like windup toys,
Until they're on the table
That's scratched with more
History than either of us —
Their beaks tap for crumbs.
But the waiter shoos them

With a dish towel.
This is a cafe for people,
Not birds, he says,
And so we leave because
We're like birds,
Transparent at love and deceit.
We hunger; we open our mouths . . .
We walk up the street, our shoes
Ringing against the stones,
To stare into a store window —
Clocks, coffee pots, an accordion
Longing for the sea.
But we're miles from the sea.
There are no boats or salt
Climbing our arms.
This is a country town,
And straw is what makes things
Go here — or so says our guidebook.
And it says that there
Is a church, lit with gold
And rare paintings,
And we start off
Hand in hand, smiling
For no reason other than
Everything is new —
The stone buildings, straw
Whacked into bundles.
What's that? my daughter
Asks, and there's no greater
Pleasure than saying,
Beats me. Let's go see.

When we bought a home in a rough area of Berkeley, the first thing I
did was plant a tree. For one, I like to watch plants grow, and for two,
our house faced a body-and-fender shop and we wanted to hide the
eyesore of dented cars.

PEPPER TREE

We tapped you into a snug hole,
Staked you to a piece
Of lumber that was once the house,
A rail from the back porch;
That, too, was a tree, cut,
Milled, and slapped with wire
For shipment, back in the thirties.
Don't worry. You're not
Going anywhere, hatrack. The wind
Comes, the sparrows come —
The rain pointless against
Your branches, notched
With a promise of leaves.
You are here, under rain
And the rain of *Get Big,* from my child.

The truth is I don't care
For the street, the banged
Cars and three-legged dogs,
The scuttle of bags
Blowing from the grocery, Lucky Day.
I don't care for the billboard,
The wires crossing and recrossing.
From the front window
I want to look at you,

Green and moving like the sea
In wind. I want you to grow
Heavy with sparrows, and if
A gull has an off day
In the weary sky, let
Your branches bear its screams,
The scraping beak. Let its wings
Open on sores, shoulders hunch,
And eyes stare me back to church.
Under this weight, that color,
Stand up, bend a little, be here tomorrow.

One of my favorite places where I live is Hinkle Park, which is known for its solitude as well as for its very large seesaws. Often, when my daughter grew bored staying inside, we would drive to this park and spread out a blanket and examine the ants, the most well-behaved insects. They never got mad when they bumped into one another.

FAILING IN THE PRESENCE OF ANTS

We live to some purpose, daughter.
Across the park, among
The trees that give the eye
Something to do, let's spread
A blanket on the ground
And examine the ants, loose
Thread to an old coat.
Perhaps they are more human than we are.
They live for the female,
Rescue their hurt, and fall earthward
For their small cause. And
Us? We live for our bellies,
The big O of our mouths.
Give me, give me, they say,
And many people, whole countries,
May go under because we desire TV
And chilled drinks, clothes
That hang well on our bodies —
Desire sofas and angled lamps,
Hair the sea may envy
On a slow day.

It is hurtful to sweep
Ants into a frenzy, blow
Chemicals into their eyes —
Those austere marchers who will lift
Their heads to rumor — seed,
Wafer of leaf, dropped apple —
And start off, over this
And that, between sloppy feet
And staggered chairs for no
Purpose other than it might be good.

Our daughter is responsible for the first sentence of this poem —
"The days are filled with air." As a poet, I am always looking and
listening, and when I heard that line, I knew immediately it had to be
mine. And it came cheaply: I bought her a donut! Now that it's in print,
I confess that it's her line.

EATING BREAD

The days are filled with air. A cloud
Over a tree. A thud of mail
In the box, and the steps of our carrier
Descending the porch. Someone is thinking
Of us, right now in the improbable heart,
And it must be good: you've chewed a smile
In your bread. "Look," you say, and I look.
I chew a smile, and press it to yours.
This is what we need. A slice
Of bread, a little quiet,
A window to sit before with our mouths full —
The neighbor kids at baseball,
A dog, that girl who could be your sister
Peeling an orange at the curb.

Daughter, though we smile with bread,
I'm troubled at not knowing what tugs the soul,
God or love, women or love,
And at how we can live in this world
With the dead itching on their racks,
A country in flames, the poor

Crouching before their banged-up bowls.
How can I tell you this? How can I show
You the men who want to hurt us all the way
To the grave. You with the hands,
The tiny teeth, the eyes that could save us
From ourselves, as right now.
You point to a bird, say "bird,"
And it lifts from a wire to a branch.
You wave, and the kids drop their gloves
To wave back. A dog looks up, a paper cup
In his mouth. Little one, tell me how this happens.

Our young daughter was always asking impossibly difficult questions. Where do the stars come from? Why is the world round? How come we sleep at night? I could answer some of the questions, and others I couldn't — like the questions about the economy of our nation.

HOW THINGS WORK

Today it's going to cost us twenty dollars
To live. Five for a softball. Four for a book,
A handful of ones for coffee and two sweet rolls,
Bus fare, rosin for your mother's violin.
We're completing our task. The tip I left
For the waitress filters down
Like rain, wetting the new roots of a child
Perhaps, a belligerent cat that won't let go
Of a balled sock until there's chicken to eat.
As far as I can tell, daughter, it works like this:
You buy bread from a grocery, a bag of apples
From a fruit stand, and what coins
Are passed on helps others buy pencils, glue,
Tickets to a movie in which laughter
Is thrown into their faces.
If we buy a goldfish, someone tries on a hat.
If we buy crayons, someone walks home with a broom.
A tip, a small purchase here and there,
And things just keep going. I guess.

I don't know how many times I have been asked what my lucky number is. When asked, I usually tell a made-up story about old men playing dominoes in a park.

FINDING A LUCKY NUMBER

When I was like you I crossed a street
To a store, and from the store
Up an alley, as I rolled chocolate
In my mouth and looked around
With my face. The day was blue
Between trees, even without wind,
And the fences were steaming
And a dog was staring into a paint bucket
And a Mexicano was raking
Spilled garbage into a box,
A raffle of eggshells and orange peels.
He nodded his head and I nodded mine
And rolled chocolate all the way
To the courthouse, where I sat
In the park, with a leaf falling
For every person who passed —
Three leaves and three daughters
With bags in their hands.
I followed them under trees,
The leaves rocking out of reach
Like those skirts I would love
From a distance. I lost them
When I bent down to tie my shoes

And begged a squirrel to eat grass.
Looking up, a dog on the run,
A grandma with a cart,
And Italians clicking dominoes
At a picnic table — men
Of the old world, in suits big enough
For Europe. I approached
Them like a squirrel, a tree
At a time, and when I was close
Enough to tell the hour from their wrists,
One laughed with hands in his hair
And turned to ask my age.
"Twelve," I said, and he knocked
My head softly with a knuckle:
"Lucky number, Sonny." He bared
His teeth, yellow and crooked
As dominoes, and tapped the front ones
With a finger. "I got twelve — see."
He opened wide until his eyes were lost
In the pouches of fat cheeks,
And I, not knowing what to do, looked in.

I've never been good at math. I know nothing about algebra, and calculus would hurt my brain. But I knew enough to begin to teach my daughter to count to one hundred.

TEACHING NUMBERS

The moon is one,
The early stars a few more . . .
The sycamore is lean
With sparrows, four perhaps,
Three hunched like hoods
And one by itself,
Wiping a beak
In the rag of its shoulder.

From where we sit
We could count to a thousand
By pointing at oranges
On trees, bright lanterns
Against the dusk, globes
Of water that won't come down.

Follow me with this, then:
A stray on two legs
At a trash can, one kite in a tree,
And a couple with four hands,
Three in pockets and one scratching
An ear busy with sound:
Door, cat, scrambling leaf.

(The world understands numbers —
At birth, you're not much
And when lowered into the earth
You're even less, a broken
Toy of 108 bones and 23 teeth
That won't stop laughing.)

But no talk of this
For the dog is happy with an eggshell
And oranges are doing wonders
At this hour in the trees
And there is popcorn to pick
From my small bowl of hands.

Let's start again,
With numbers that will help.

The moon is one,
The early stars a few more . . .

For years I wasn't happy, but one day I woke up and began to believe more in the simplicity of a rose, a peach tree, the sun hanging over a roof, and the sheer freedom of getting up and walking around.

LOOKING AROUND, BELIEVING

How strange that we can begin at any time.
With two feet we get down the street.
With a hand we undo the rose.
With an eye we lift up the peach tree
And hold it up to the wind — white blossoms
At our feet. Like today. I started
In the yard with my daughter,
With my wife poking at a potted geranium,
And now I am walking down the street,
Amazed that the sun is only so high,
Just over the roof, and a child
Is singing through a rolled newspaper
And a terrier is leaping like a flea
And at the bakery I pass, a palm
Like a suctioning starfish is pressed
To the window. We're keeping busy —
This way, that way, we're making shadows
Where sunlight was, making words
Where there was only noise in the trees.

Because I grew up poor, I sometimes feel that I should share my childhood stories with my daughter, especially at the dinner table. She's heard a good number of my stories, and is bored silly.

EVENING WALK

My daughter runs outside to busy
Herself with tiny cakes of mud.
"It's important," she says,
Not wanting to hear my poor stories again.
Still I drag her to the car
And the short climb to the Berkeley
Hills, for gardens are in bloom,
Red thing and yellow this and that.
Trees with rootfuls of clouds
Line the walk. "They're older than me,"
I say, and she won't look at them
Or the grandma houses,
Quaint as tea cups.

The rich seem never to come out
Of their houses. They never sit on
Lawns, or bang a ball against
The garage door, or water the green strip
Along the street — hose in one hand,
Can of beer in the other.
At our place, the flowers fall
When we turn a hose on them
  — even the pepper tree, rigged

With wire and rope, fell over
Like the neck of a sick giraffe.

I talk and talk. I say the poor
Rave about the color orange
And the rich yammer over egg-white.
I put this to Mariko, steps ahead,
A plucked branch dragging in her hand,
And begin again, a bore to the end.
When I was like you, I picked
Grapes like nobody's business . . .
She starts to skip. I walk faster,
Loud as a fool. When I was a kid,
I lugged oranges and shared plums with Okies . . .
But she's on the run, the branch
Fluttering like a green fire
Because the corner is up ahead
And an evening without me
Can't be far beyond.

QUESTIONS AND ANSWERS ABOUT POETRY

Q *Where do your poems come from?*

A They come from my memory or from a story someone told me; they come from feelings and the inventive side of the mind. Most of the poems in this collection come from real experiences. But, like other artists, I treat the experiences with a measure of creativity.

Q *Then, not everything in your narrative poems is true?*

A No. But most poets who tell stories through verse believe that poems should be credible, that the experiences in them should be possible in life even if they did not happen to the poet. For instance, in "Learning to Bargain," my friend didn't really kill the cat. As I remember, he heaved a brick at it because it had knocked over his garbage can. Luckily, he missed. Still, I didn't like the idea of his trying to hurt the cat. I threatened to tell his mom if he ever did it again. In the poem, I make our actions more ominous. I say that he killed the cat and that I threatened to tell unless he paid me a dime. I wanted to show in the poem how people start conspiring at a very early age.

Q *Do all poems tell stories?*

A No. A lyric poem expresses the feelings or thoughts of the poem's speaker. (The speaker does not have to be the poet.) A lyric poem does not tell a complete story, as a narrative poem does. "October" is a lyric poem.

Q *Do you have to get inspired to write?*

A When I began writing fifteen years ago, I waited to be "inspired," which for me was a physical sensation — my body tingled. Now I get this feeling less frequently. I doodle a few phrases or lines, and a nice feeling settles on my shoulders. This is a sign that I'm ready to write. It's the same with an artist friend. Sometimes she doesn't know what she's going to paint until she sketches a few lines, maybe a face, maybe an outline of a tree. Then, suddenly, like the flash of a camera, she has an idea and a feeling settles on her shoulders, too.

Q *When do you write?*

A Each poet has a routine. I write in the summer when I'm not teaching, and I write in the morning because my mind is clear and I can concentrate. After breakfast, I go out to my garage, which I've turned into a study, and write for two or three hours; then I have lunch, and do something else in the afternoon. When I'm stuck on a line, I go to the bench press in the backyard and do a quick set of reps, which is usually enough to get the blood and my imagination going.

Q *Do you have to change any of your words?*

A Since most poems are short, compared to other kinds of literature, every line needs a great deal of attention. I once worked on a single fourteen-line poem for a week, changing verbs, reworking line breaks, cutting out unnecessary words.

Q *Do you have a favorite poem?*

A Yes, but don't tell my other poems. My favorite is "Hitchhiking With a Friend and a Book That Explains the Pacific Ocean." The poem is about wonderment. I had never hitchhiked in my life when a friend, also named Gary, suggested that we hitchhike to the ocean. We stood at the edge of a road outside Fresno and waited and waited. Two hours later a truck driver picked us up, took us a short distance, and dropped us off near a dairy. After a short wait there, a man in a banged-up truck picked us up.

Q *Do you write the titles of your poems first?*

A I usually come up with a title when I'm about halfway through a poem. A title often hints to the reader what the poem is about. At times, however, poets will use wild titles that they may not wholly understand but may like for the way they sound or the way they look on the page.

Q *Why are poems difficult to understand?*

A Poetry is a concentrated form of writing; so much meaning is packed into such a little space. Therefore, each word in a poem is very important and is chosen very carefully to convey just the right meaning. For example, the word *tree* might *stand* for more than a tree in an orchard. It might symbolize life itself, or it might symbolize the strength of your grandfather or your father. *Rain* may symbolize tears; *dusk* may symbolize approaching death.

Another reason why poetry can be difficult to understand is that you're not used to reading it. The more you read it, the better you get at understanding words and lines.

Q *Should I read a poem more than once?*

A Yes, by all means. Read it again and again. One poet remarked that "poetry is an act of attention" — you have to concentrate when you read a poem, just as you must concentrate when you're in the batter's box and your team needs you to bring in a player on second base.

I also like to think of a poem as a new person. Just because you say hello once doesn't mean that you never want to see this person again. Of course you do. A poem also needs to be seen again and again.

Q *Why don't your poems rhyme?*

A Most poets today don't use rhyme; they write "free verse" — poetry that has no regular rhyme or rhythm. Poetry has changed over the years, but poets' motives for writing poetry haven't changed. Most poets write because they feel something and want to share it with others.

Q *When did you decide to become a poet?*

A I decided to become a poet after I read a funny/sad poem by Edward Field called "Unwanted." It's about a lonely man who feels sad that no one wants him. He hangs a picture of himself at the post office next to posters of dangerous criminals. He wants people to recognize him and love him. I was inspired by this poem and identified with it because it seemed to speak about my own life. I read the poem over and over, and even typed it out to see what it looked like. I read this poet's book and began to read other poets. After a while, I decided to write my own poems, and I have been doing it ever since.

ABOUT THE AUTHOR

GARY SOTO teaches at the University of California at Berkeley. His poems have appeared in many magazines including the *New Yorker* and *Poetry*. He is the author of three books for young adults: *Baseball in April*, *A Summer Life*, and *Taking Sides*. During his free time Gary likes to read, travel, play basketball, and do volunteer work for a local Boys' Club, where he teaches karate.

Gary Soto lives with his wife and daughter and the three family cats, Pip, Groucho, and Corky, in Albany, California.